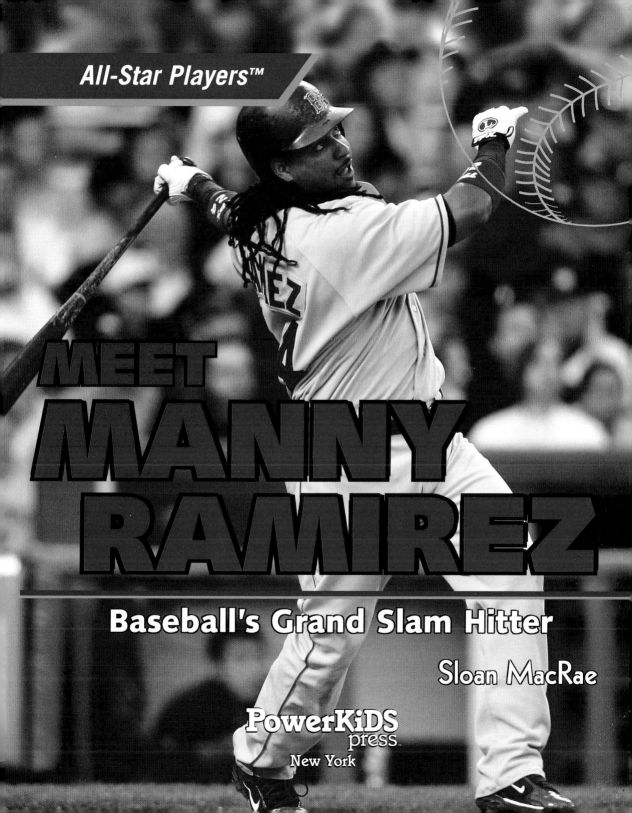

All-Star Players™

MEET MANNY RAMIREZ

Baseball's Grand Slam Hitter

Sloan MacRae

PowerKiDS press

New York

Published in 2009 by The Rosen Publishing Group, Inc.
29 East 21st Street, New York, NY 10010

First Edition

Editor: Amelie von Zumbusch
Book Design: Greg Tucker
Photo Researcher: Jessica Gerweck

Photo Credits: Cover, pp. 5, 13, 14, 17, 18, 19, 20, 22, 23, 25, 26, 27, 29, 30 © Getty Images; pp. 6, 9, 11, 12 © MLB Photos via Getty Images.

Library of Congress Cataloging-in-Publication Data

MacRae, Sloan.
   Meet Manny Ramirez : baseball's grand slam hitter / Sloan MacRae. — 1st ed.
      p. cm. — (All-star players)
   Includes index.
   ISBN 978-1-4358-2708-0 (library binding) — ISBN 978-1-4358-3100-1 (pbk.)
ISBN 978-1-4358-3106-3 (6-pack)
   1. Ramirez, Manny, 1972– —Juvenile literature. 2. Baseball players—United States—Biography—Juvenile literature. I. Title.
   GV865.R38M33 2009
   796.357092—dc22
   [B]
                                                2008022383

Manufactured in the United States of America

Contents

Ramirez is one of the best baseball players in Major League Baseball, or MLB. He has played left field for the Los Angeles Dodgers, the Boston Red Sox, and the Cleveland Indians. However, Ramirez is often **criticized** for behaving strangely. Some people think Manny Ramirez seems crazy. Others find him childish. Ramirez's fans enjoy the oddball side of him, though.

Ramirez's fans and critics both agree that he is one of the best hitters of all time. Ramirez has hit more **postseason** home runs than any other player in the history of baseball! He knows that you cannot help what others think of you. You can only do your best. Ramirez's best is very good.

All-Star Facts

Ramirez's full name is Manuel Aristides Ramírez, but people have called him Manny for years.

Manny Ramirez's laid-back nature has won him many fans. Other fans were won over by his astounding skill as a hitter.

Washington Heights

In 1972, Manny Ramirez was born in the Dominican Republic, a country in the Caribbean. His parents moved to the United States when he was 13. Manny and his three sisters stayed in the Dominican Republic with relatives. Two years later, the Ramirez children joined their parents.

The family lived in New York City, in a neighborhood called Washington Heights. Many **immigrants** from the Dominican Republic live in Washington Heights. There were several baseball fields in Washington Heights, and Ramirez became the neighborhood star. Manny led his high-school baseball team to three Manhattan Division championships. He was named the Public Schools Athletic League High School Player of the Year.

Ramirez is proud of his Dominican background. Here, he is carrying the flag of the Dominican Republic.

Ramirez finished high school and was **drafted** by the Cleveland Indians. However, he had to prove himself in the minor leagues before he could play MLB baseball. There are several levels of minor-league teams. Most minor-league players never make it to the majors. Ramirez **ascended** through the minor leagues quickly.

On September 2, 1993, Ramirez played his first major-league game for the Cleveland Indians. He did not get any hits. However, Ramirez played much better in his second major-league game. He hit two home runs and a double against his hometown team, the New York Yankees. Ramirez was in the majors to stay!

Ramirez went on to play for the Cleveland Indians in a total of 22 games in 1993.

The 1994 season was supposed to be Ramirez's first whole season with the Cleveland Indians. Unfortunately, the major-league players went on **strike**. The season was short, and Ramirez did not get to play in many games. He still hit lots of home runs, though.

Ramirez came back in 1995 and became a star. His batting average was .308. A batting average is a number that tells how good a batter is. A batting average above .280 is considered pretty good, and Ramirez's .308 average was very good. Ramirez's .308 average meant that he got about 3 hits in every 10 trips to the plate.

Ramirez played so well in 1994 that he was the runner-up for the Rookie of the Year award. An MLB player's rookie year is the first year he plays regularly in the major leagues.

Manny Ramirez had a great year in 1995. His wonderful hitting helped win the Indians a spot in the World Series for the first time in 41 years.

That year, Ramirez also hit 31 home runs. He knocked in 107 RBIs, too. "RBI" stands for "run batted in." RBIs happen when a batter's hits let his teammates score. Ramirez helped his teammates score 107 runs in the season. His RBIs would soon make him famous.

Ramirez helped the Indians reach the postseason five years in a row. He even led them to the World Series in 1995 and in 1997. The World Series is the championship of baseball. Unfortunately, the Indians lost the World Series both times.

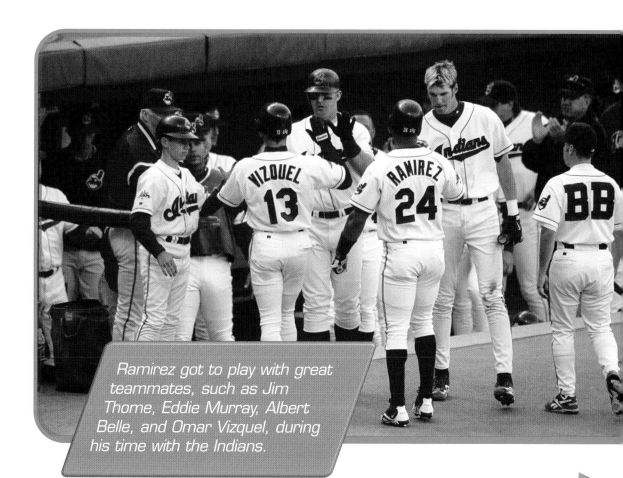

Ramirez got to play with great teammates, such as Jim Thome, Eddie Murray, Albert Belle, and Omar Vizquel, during his time with the Indians.

A Home-Run Machine

Ramirez did not win any championships for the Indians, but he did become one of the best players in baseball. His fame grew, and he recorded some of the best **stats** in the majors. In 1999, Ramirez collected 165 RBIs. No one had knocked in this many runs in one season since 1938!

Ramirez enjoyed playing for the Indians, but he was ready for a change. The Boston Red Sox were trying to put together a team that would win the World Series. They needed a great home-run hitter. The Red Sox paid Ramirez $160 million to be their new home-run machine.

While he was playing for the Cleveland Indians, Ramirez hit a total of 236 home runs!

Ramirez was excited to play for the Red Sox because he believed they could win the World Series. Many baseball **experts** and fans disagreed, though. The Boston Red Sox had not won a World Series since 1918. That was the year that they traded Babe Ruth to the Yankees. Many people believe Babe Ruth was the greatest baseball player who ever lived. His nickname was "the Bambino." Baseball fans thought the Red Sox brought bad luck on themselves when they traded Ruth away and believed they would never win the World Series again because of the Curse of the Bambino.

In 2004, both Ramirez and the Red Sox made baseball history. Ramirez led the American League in home runs. The Red Sox reached the

After joining the Red Sox, Ramirez continued to wear number 24, the number he had worn when he played for the Indians.

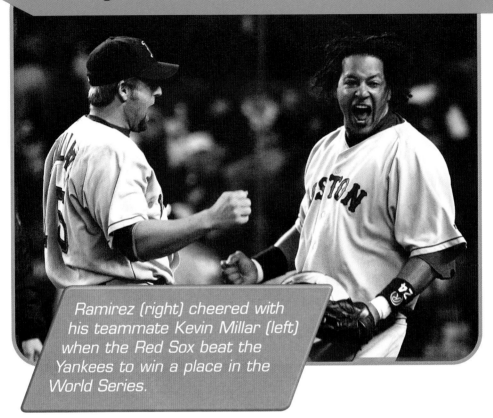

Ramirez (right) cheered with his teammate Kevin Millar (left) when the Red Sox beat the Yankees to win a place in the World Series.

postseason, but they lost the first three games of the American League Championship Series to the Yankees. No major-league team had ever come back from such a **deficit**. However, the Red Sox did! They **rallied** and won the next four games to beat the Yankees. Then the Red Sox went on to **sweep** the St. Louis Cardinals in the World Series.

Ramirez was named the World Series Most Valuable Player, or MVP. This meant that baseball experts thought Ramirez was the best player on either team in the World Series. He had helped break the Curse of the Bambino!

Ramirez was the first Red Sox player ever to be named the World Series MVP!

Ramirez has hit more grand slams than any other MLB player who is playing today.

Ramirez was not finished making baseball history. He hit his four hundredth home run in 2005. At the time, only 38 other players had ever done this. Ramirez hit his twentieth grand slam in the same season. A grand slam happens when a batter hits a home run when the bases are loaded. The bases are loaded when there are runners on every base. Only the baseball **legend** Lou Gehrig had ever hit more than 20 grand slams. Experts even think Ramirez may break Gehrig's record of 23 grand slams someday!

The Red Sox reached the World Series again in 2007, but Ramirez did not have a great season.

All-Star Facts

Ramirez was on the cover of the video game MVP Baseball 2005, by EA Sports. This is a big honor for a player.

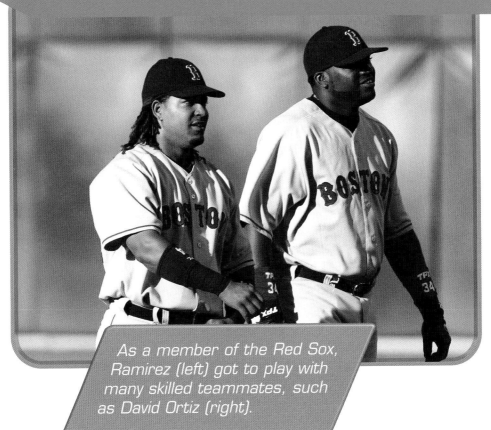

As a member of the Red Sox, Ramirez (left) got to play with many skilled teammates, such as David Ortiz (right).

During the regular season, his batting average was .296, and he hit 20 home runs. Many major-league players would consider this a great season, but Ramirez knew he could play better. In fact, he did play much better in the postseason. Ramirez's twenty-third career postseason home run broke the major-league record held by Bernie Williams of the Yankees. The Red Sox went on to sweep the Colorado Rockies in the World Series. Many of the greatest baseball stars never win a single World Series. Ramirez has won two and could win more.

Ramirez and the Red Sox beat the Rockies, 4–3, on October 28, 2007, to win their second World Series in just four years.

Manny Being Manny

Sometimes Ramirez's actions make his fans nervous. Ramirez has a **reputation** for not always paying attention. Fenway Park, where the Red Sox play, has a green outfield wall that is called the Green Monster. Ramirez has been known to disappear behind the Green Monster during games and show up again only at the last minute. He has listened to music on an MP3 player built into his sunglasses while he was playing left field, too. Fans call this behavior Manny being Manny. Ramirez does not seem to mind that people think he is **eccentric**.

Ramirez is not always carefree. He is serious about helping people, especially children. Ramirez

Manny Ramirez is one of the easiest MLB players to spot. He is known for playing in a baggy uniform and wearing his hair in dreadlocks.

Here, Manny Ramirez and his son, also called Manny, are spending time together after a batting practice.

often teaches children how to play baseball. He shows them how to become better batters. Ramirez created his own **charity** to help children in need. He often works with an organization called CHARLEE. CHARLEE helps children who have been abused, or treated badly. Ramirez once raised money for CHARLEE by selling a kind of wine, called Manny Being Merlot.

Ramirez also helped others when floods hit the Dominican Republic in 2004 and many people living there lost everything they owned. Ramirez was troubled that life was so hard for people in

Manny Ramirez met his wife, Juliana, at a gym. Juliana comes from Brazil.

his home country. He and his teammates donated money to help the **victims**.

The 500 Club

Ramirez hit his five hundredth home run in 2008. At that time, only 23 other players had ever hit 500 or more home runs. These players are called the 500 Club. Ramirez's great home-run record means that, after he retires, he will probably reach the Hall of Fame. The National Baseball Hall of Fame and Museum is a museum in Cooperstown, New York. Luckily for his fans, Ramirez is not likely to retire soon.

The summer of 2008 brought big changes for Ramirez. In late July, he was traded to a new team, the Los Angeles Dodgers. Who knows what records he will break with them?

Ramirez got off to a great start with his new team. He hit three home runs in his first five games with the Dodgers.

Height: 6' (1.8 m)
Weight: 200 pounds (91 kg)
Position: Left field
Bats: Right
Throws: Right
Date of Birth: May 30, 1972

2007 Season Stats

At Bats	Runs	Hits	Home Runs	RBIs	Batting Average
483	84	143	20	88	.296

Career Stats as of October 2007

At Bats	Runs	Hits	Home Runs	RBIs	Batting Average
7,058	1,342	2,209	490	1,604	.304

Glossary

ascended (un-SEND-ed) Moved upward.

charity (CHER-uh-tee) A group that gives help to the needy.

criticized (KRIH-tuh-syzd) Found fault with.

deficit (DEH-fuh-sut) The amount of something that needs to be made up.

drafted (DRAFT-ed) Selected for a special purpose.

eccentric (ik-SEN-trik) Strange, different from established ways or styles.

experts (EK-sperts) People who know a lot about a subject.

immigrants (IH-muh-grunts) People who moved to a new country from another country.

legend (LEH-jend) A person who has been famous and honored for a very long time.

postseason (pohst-SEE-zun) Games played after the regular season.

rallied (RA-leed) Recovered strength, energy, or health.

reputation (reh-pyoo-TAY-shun) The ideas people have about another person, an animal, or an object.

stats (STATS) Facts about players in the form of numbers.

strike (STRYK) A refusal to work until changes are made.

sweep (SWEEP) To win all stages of a game or contest.

victims (VIK-timz) People or animals that have been harmed or killed.

Index

Web Sites

Due to the changing nature of Internet links, PowerKids Press has developed an online list of Web sites related to the subject of this book. This site is updated regularly. Please use this link to access the list:
www.powerkidslinks.com/asp/mannyr/